GUNJAN GUJRAL

Poems & Thoughts

Illustrations by Vipul Panchal

Typeset and designed at Tulika Print Communication Services, 35A/1, Third Floor, Shahpur Jat, New Delhi

Printed at Pauls Press, E44/1, Okhla Phase II, New Delhi 110 020

ISBN 81-87943-09-2 Pages : 106 Price : Rs. 195/-

India Research Press, B-4/22, Safdarjung Enclave, New Delhi - 110029

Contents

Acknowledgement

We are sincerely grateful to all the people who have contributed in bringing out this work by Gunjan. We are especially grateful to Shri Deepak Chaturvedi, Shri Ashish Tyagi and Shri Sameep Nanda who have worked very hand and without whose encouragement and support it would not have been possible to bring out this book. We also thank Dr Satya Dev Jaggi who went through Gunjan's work and gave us the encouragement and confidence to get it published.

Kamini and Rajender Gujral
(Gunjan's parents)

Foreword

I first met Gunjan when she was but a child, in Maiduguri (Nigeria), where I was a teacher in the Department of English and her father in the Department of Physics, in the University of Maiduguri. She impressed me as a very promising child in many ways. I dedicated a set of poems I wrote in my first year of stay in Maiduguri, under the title *Far in Maiduguri,* to her and two other children who had impressed me likewise. I hoped that when the three children grew up they would recall with nostalgia some aspects of life in Maiduguri and that they would be intrigued to compare their own recollections with my evocation of them in verse. In fact, I presented Gunjan a copy of *Far in Maiduguri* more than fifteen years after its publication. But before she could communicate any specific reaction to me, she was no more. She died of cancer after she had been treated and apparently cured.

A pleasant surprise was in store for me when recently her parents handed me a set of her poems and articles for my evaluation and comments. I was thoroughly impressed. On reading her writings, I realized that she was indeed the kind of person to whom one may dedicate a set of poems. I feel sad that so much of what these pieces promise will remain for ever unfulfilled: there is, in the best among them, the makings of an Emily Dickinson or an Arundhati Roy. But I am glad that these pieces are there and that they are going to be published and circulated, as they deserve to be.

In these writings Gunjan evokes many exciting events and amusing personae, especially relating to her life in school and college. A school or college student would find in many of these a reflection of his own experiences. At the same time, they would stimulate them to achieve the larger vision that makes for a sense of maturity and responsibility in the context of the adult world.

Gunjan states her inexpressible love for her father in terms that are simple yet final, needing no analysis. She makes a close and critical observation of the varied species of boys, in and out of love, and in and out of fashion. Despite her habitual kindness, her welcome of guests munching 'on your delicious biscuits' is tinged with irony. She responds to Valentine's Day as an expression of the human longing for love, as fulfilling an urgent and basic human need. She is not averse to being critical of those whose commitment to life is only in terms of fun. She recalls, in a poem, the amusing hypocrisy of those who loudly proclaim allegiance to school studies and yet are ever ready to flout its rules of discipline, taking delight only in the possibilities of fun at school. In 'Shoe Mania' she conjures up a funny picture of her sister for whom a passion for shoes outdoes all other considerations. She also paints an amusing picture of her 'philosophical uncle' to whom Gandhi and Mandela are fools, and who is yet the 'sweetest person in the whole world'. In 'Free Period' she describes the dilemma of students who love their free periods but lament that the free periods must soon end.

She portrays love in a number of poems — generally in a lighter vein and sometimes as tragic. Occasionally it begins in laughter and ends in tears. Taken responsibly, love to her is a generator of values; the mutuality of a love relationship is a supreme source of values. She is a keen observer of the subtle differences between expressing and affirming true love and being a flirt. Strengthening faith and rekindling hope, love to her must eventually turn into a larger vision which emphasizes those elements in life that complement rather than contradict each other, which brings people together rather than separates and divides them. The antitheses of love — hate, scorn, anger, contempt, rancour leading to disillusionment, frustration, discouragement — all these add up to a startling toll of emotional and moral illness in the world. Love, on the other hand, lends exposure to concepts that are elevating and invigorating. It expands our horizons such that our habitual gloom begins to lighten and our ingrained hardness of the heart begins to soften.

Most of Gunjan's poems appeal not only to feelings but arouse the imagination and stimulate intellectual debate at levels higher than the mind. They condense significant essential principles into a form easily impressed upon the memory, trying to make precise, in the words of a poet:

> What simply sparkled in men's eyes before,
> Twitched in their brow or quivered on their lips,
> Waited to speech they called but would not come.

She has no use for virtues that stunt the personality, preventing one from making full use of one's potentialities. She evokes a world of affection and loyalties, of vision and ideas, of devotion and sacrifice. She plucks at her poetic strings with just the touch that the human heart craves, sensitive to personal outcries wrung from the heart in the intense twists and turns of life.

The voice that emerges from these poems is that of a very humane person seeking to satisfy the various kinds of hunger that are a part of everyone's make-up rather than simply superimpose on herself and others the various courses of reformation suggested by history. As has been well said, there is no power so hard to cultivate and keep as a kind voice.

While evoking the restless world of young people, Gunjan expresses her belief that certain ways of living and thinking and feeling are better than others — ways that are conducive to the creation of harmony and justice and peace, ways that intensify our aspiration towards the good and the beautiful. She discovers a great deal in life, in all that surrounds us, that truly warms and touches the heart. Yet she seeks to raise the level of our consciousness by helping us to see our commitments in the context of God's presumed expectations of us. She seeks to instil in us a sense of the presence of God in everything and everywhere, as making possible all good things in life, presiding over mankind as a single community and forever goading it to realize itself as a single family. Nature to her is a gift from God, and its beauties are an expression of God's infinite power and infinite compassion.

From the above discussion of her work, we can see only too well how lasting Gunjan's contribution might have been but for her untimely exit from the stage of this world.

11 November 2001 — Dr Satya Dev Jaggi
New Delhi

Remembering Gunjan

Six years of knowing Gunj in a small li'l para seemed next to impossible. I could go on and on and a write a whole book or make a movie on it. Still cant forget the first day we met—Times FM office and she was sitting on My seat. But days went on and I became the producer of her show and started recording more and more with her. I guess thats how it began—the story of getting to know someone as bright, inteligent, and as witty as Gunj. She always reminded me of the Solitary Reaper or the Highland Lass—tossing her hair and enjoying each moment and as if she were part of nature itself (she loved the hills thats what she always said). Some popular quotes from Gunj herself:

"I love to eat"

"I love Amitabh and he's from Sherwood too"

"I love my Pepsi" (its not an endorsement)

"I love Kebabs and my mom makes the best Shaami's" (which is true)

"HCF (Hot Chocolate Fudge) is the best thing that could've happened"

"I love to act and I' think I'd do the old timer roles like Meena Kumari's very well"

"I can sleep anywhere, anytime" (don't we all know)

"What yaaaa—"

Well, I could go on and on. I guess knowing Gunj was the best thing that could've happened to me or I guess to any one of us. Each moment spent with her, though now seems more like a dream—will always remain in each one of our hearts. She managed to make her place in it even if she met you for the least possible time. The questions will always remain—Why? Why her? She didn't do anybody no harm? This was not her time to go? This is just not fair? I personally wouldn't believe in anyone up there–but after whatever she went through—she faced it all with a smile, and I guess thats how we should all remember her as. These articles and poems and her paintings are just a small example of what Gunj was all about, what she experienced right from school to college to what all she was going through during her treatment. A small li'l endeavour to always remember her with a smile, cos thats what she would have wanted—For everyone to be happy. She came, she saw and now she's gone but she'll always be there for those who believed in her. In every face or gesture, you'll be reminded of her in some way or the other—but that's ok who wants to let go of a sweet memory like Gunj. Enjoy getting to know her.

Sameep
(Gunjan's friend)

* * *

"Good friends are for keeps"
Is what she said to me,
She is the friend I knew,
Who spoke words very few.
Her thoughts were penned in her books,
With colours and hues her mind flowed on a
Canvas or two.
In theater and movies she did her part well,
She deserved an Oscar is what we all said.
Her radiant smile warmed many a heart,

Like a gentle breeze did she part.
And for her I say the same, "Good friends are for keeps",
She is the friend I have for keeps.

Rima Sukhija
(Gunjan's friend)

* * *

My earliest memory of Gunjan is when she had come for holidays from Nigeria to Delhi. She was about 4 years old then. We were running and she tripped and shouted "Girti Hoon". Is not it ironical that the first words I remember of our most prolific writer were in broken Hindi. As a kid, her favorite pass time was sitting alone in our courtyard dressed as a bride. In Retrospect, that was the portrait of a very talented individual content with life and happy in solitude. Above all, I remember my little sister as some one I would bribe with Chinese lunch to accompany me, some one with whom I could sit and talk for hours, but most importantly some one I would never see again.

Rohit Gujral
(Gunjan's cousin)

* * *

Gunjan—"a rose in the wilderness" somebody had just used the phrase off hand for her—not with any deep thought—just a spontaneous remark which indeed is apt for her. A mixture of intelligence, confidence, creativity, sensitivity and a child like innocence—so very different from the modern youth. A short meeting with her could have an everlasting impact.

I can still not get down to using the term 'was' for Gunjan as she is so much with all of us even now. But the fact is slowly sinking in that God had given this 'gift' to us on loan for a very short perod of time.

One does not know intimately all the cousins that one has but Gunjan is more like a child for me—she stayed with me a lot as I was her local guardian in her Hindu College days. Infact she even gave me a card on 'Mothers' Day' a couple of years back. In the family she was the ultimate in looks and academics in her age group of children. Always doing so well in school—acting in plays, writing in the Dailies then being the headgirl in Sherwood followed by Graduation in one of the best Colleges in Delhi University. Next what we hear is that Gunjan is on Air on Times FM—speaking her heart out and acquiring fans.

With a big blow of fate the disaster struck—the agony of over two years did not shake the dignity of this Child—looking beautiful till the end she just slipped away from our hands.

The closeness of her friends with the family even now only proves Gunjan's spiritual presence. She will be with us forever.

Madhu Arora

(Gunjan's cousin)

* * *

Gunjan, the sunshine of our lives. . . .she was always smiling no matter what! She made me a "sister", a very proud and happy one. I always Felt this bond with her which is hard to explain. All I know is that she left a void within me, which no body can ever fill. My little sunshine, my babydoll will always be there wherever I go. I ask thee that I be united with her after my life here on this earth is over. Gunjan, my jann, God's special angel shall always look over us and I shall do my best to fulfill her dreams.

Nidhi

(Gunjan's sister)

* * *

Beautiful, simple and very smart. That was our Gunjino. Who will always be with us and our children to come. . . .Gunjan for me was a sister and friend and I will never forget.

Abderrazak
(Gunjan's brother-in-law)

* * *

Gunjan, a daughter full of love and affection. I always think of her as a good friend. She was quick in understanding people's behaviour, so kindness and consideration came to her naturally. She had an excellent sense of humour. Her smile was infectious. Grace was part of her and it never left her even during the toughest treatment she went through. She has given me a life full of happiness. She was like a bud blooming in to a beautiful flower. She will ALWAYS be with me giving strength to do something Worthwhile in her name.

Kamini Gujral
(Gunjan's mother)

* * *

Gunjan started to show interest in writing poems, painting and performing in plays when she was about five or six years of age. She was a shy and reserved child, but would turn into a confident and uninhibted performer in front of audience. As she got older, what amazed me so often was this uncanny quality to observe detail in surroundings and people around and to express it instantly in form of simple verse or prose with which you could identify immediately. Most of her writings are results of such instant reaction of happenings in real life. I remember she wrote "Unwanted Guests" when some friends of our turned up at midnight unannounced. "Shoe Mania" was written when she found her sister arranging her shoes and looking dejected when a pair seemed worn out. Another quality of her's was ability to see some humour in the most annoying or depressing situations. For example when her sister or brother would be heart-broken she would come up with a "Being in Love".

But as she grew, her writings took on a more serious colour.

Perhaps as a child she could not communicate with me as much as she would have liked, may be because of my reserved nature. But she knew how much I loved her and cared for her. She expresses these sentiments very simply but touchingly in "For Papa", a verse she got frammed and presented me on my 50th birthday. Many of her writings in later years of her life—a short life of twenty-four years, turned towards exploring her relationship with God. Gunjan's biggest strength was hope. She faught her decease with a single mindedness in the hope that she would get well and go on with life God wished otherwise I am sure you will enjoy reading these compositions. One can identify with most of the characters and incidents in these writings at some stage of one's life, wether as a child, a teenager or a middle aged parent.

Rajender Gujral
(Gunjan's father)

POEMS

For Papa

You led my tiny feet
Held my little hand
Through mud, snow and sand.
I know we haven't spoken much
But both of us know, don't we,
In all this world I Love one most of all
Papa that is You.

The Varied Species

You'll see them here,
You'll see them there,
Up, down and everywhere.
A dozen species, or maybe more,
A thesis on them would excite even a bore.
One boy each to suit your mood,
There are some who are kind, others extremely rude.
Some are intelligent, some oh! so dumb,
Some so handsome, on seeing whom you'd go numb.
Lets call one 'A', he's liberal, free as a dove,
To every girl he swears his love.
But beware friends, sisters and girls,
He's actually neither yours, nor hers.
Then there's that not so smart Mr. 'B'.
On seeing a girl he shouts with glee.
Good in studies perhaps but better at this.
Then there is the semi-smart type, Mr. 'C'—
Spectacles and the laws of Newton are his very being,
You pity him greatly, for what he's obviously missing.
Then there's 'X' a roadside Romeo, on the streets,
You may scorn him now, offer him no bus seat,

But when he becomes a star, a-la Ajay Devgan and
shines on the screen,
You'd curse yourself for having been so mean.
Mr. 'Y' is sophisticated sort and rich,
Any boy would like to switch his roles with his.
The girls keep waiting, for there's a hitch,
Once your heart is torn to pieces, he isn't there to
mend or stitch it.
Then there's the shy, introvert, smart Mr. 'Z',
But so attached to his mother there's not much to say
To anyone but her
Don't lose heart girls, you might find your match
In a nearly perfect creation, who will not be snatched
away.
That's rare, though.
If God hasn't spent hours making you,
You might as well pick up an A or a C
For haven't you heard the little saying,
None is perfect in this world
They and we are just examples,
Of the numberless humans we daily see and meet.

Reflection

Puddles on the pathway
Each holds a moon
Dark, brooding, grey.
Beautiful, anyway
Each telling of a lore—
Love, strange and stifling
With just a single person
Or with many more
There are puddles with half the moon
Like an unwanted bride
Deprived, desolate,
Waiting endlessly for the groom.
The puddles dry
The Moon has nowhere to go
Is it so?
It rests on a door, or a window
Love finds its way
Love rests someday
On a single person, on a single soul.

In Sherwood School

To each girl there is a boy,
Whether he's smart, cute or coy.
But the ratio here is quite alarming,
And rather disarming.
The guys will do anything for these girls, you know,
For them all their money blow,
Buy them flowers, shower them with love,
Too scared, that they'll fly away like a dove.
But sooner or later, the time arrives,
The girl leaves the guy, however much he strives.
However much he begs, or pleads,
Women's liberation coming into force, the girl walks
    away and pays little heed.
Here in Sherwood, as I mentioned before,
For every girl there are ten guys or maybe more,
Everywhere else in the world, the girl has to
    compromise,
But here she is growing wise,
Having always her way,
The girls have quite an upper hand,
They just have to give a smile to work the magic wand,
The guys come running, all in flattery,

Perhaps it would be too strong, to call it 'slavery',
But when I say this, you know what I mean,
Since I've joined Sherwood
On my face there is always an unearthly gleam!

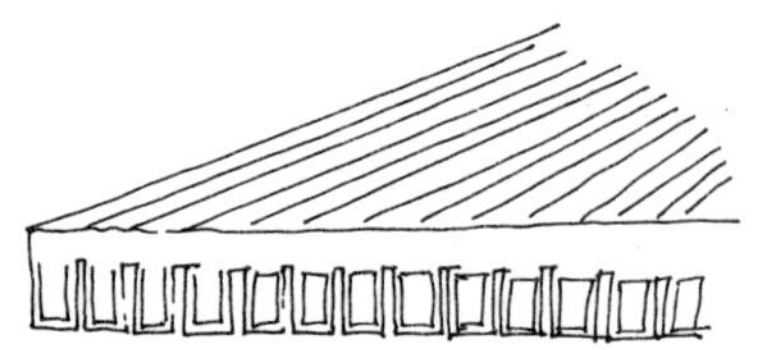

Being in Love

Being in Love,
It's a funny thing,
You dance and howl and laugh and sing.
All at once I've seen my sister and my brother,
When in love, being out of their mind.
To all else blind.
Love is all to them,
God isn't there anymore.
When they talk to U, they seem to believe you're a big
bore,
How worried are they at not receiving letters.
Nourishing always fear of being deceived.
Sad music, sad movies and of course phone calls
Are all they call their own.
Their love is going to call, you see.
They are even more foolish than they seem.
They may wake up and exclaim, "Oh shucks"!
What a fool I've been,
To have loved someone like her or him,
It's really beyond belief,
What with their parental efforts could not come to cease,
Is oft achieved by a common friend,

Saying such cruel words you see,
"I think your lover or beloved loves only me"

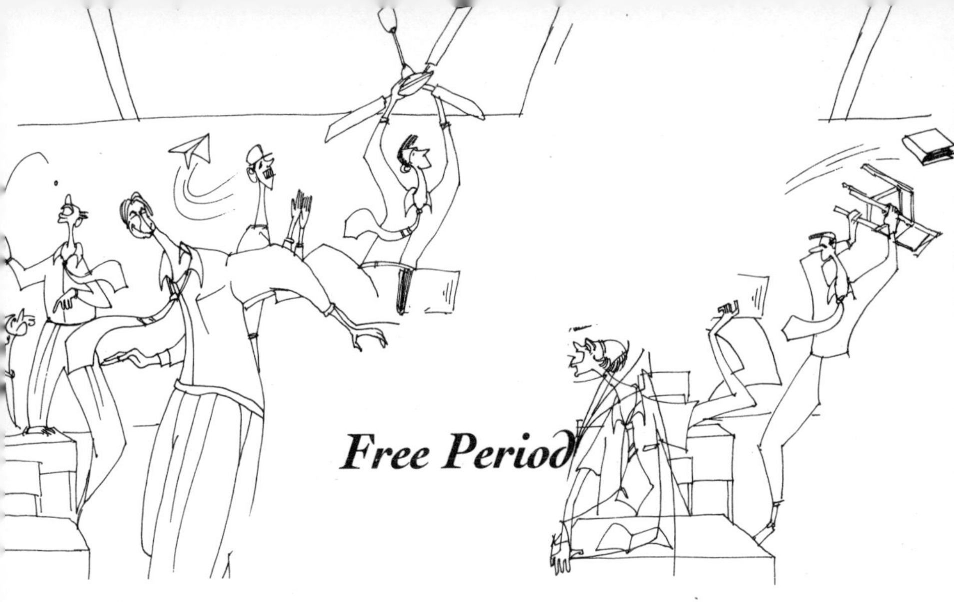

Free Period

"Which period is this, please tell me that"–
Another one shouts, 'I'm really out of track'.
It's a classroom scene you see,
The buzzing is louder than that of bees.
The girls are shouting and screaming,
Though there are some who are dreaming
It's rare to find such a merry gleam
On every face, as in a classroom.
The usual faces seen are so dull,
When studying Shakespeare or a skull.
But for now such things left behind,
Fun n' frolic are on every mind.
Soon the teacher's bell will toll
For girls to learn the bitter truth,
Each free period comes to an End.

The Messiah of Love

Remembering him today,
There is a great deal we can say,
But above all this
That he was one of the finest men,
Task of building up a crumbled nation,
His sole ambition.
True, honest, intelligent, wise,
Honoured by his country and the world.
In love above all with the children,
They still flock to him, to gain his love,
A drop from his sea of love,
Which he showers still on the whole world,
As on his beloved country.

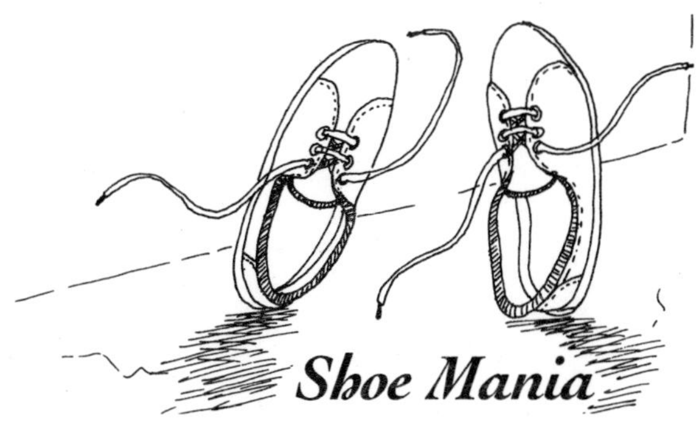

Shoe Mania

She treats them with so much care, all her love is
showered on them,
From the time they are born till they are at least seven.
During the course of their long-lived life,
She's a mother to them, a sister and a wife.
My sister and her shoes are what I'm talking about.
Her concern for them
Leaves her love for us humans in doubt.
Once she has acquired a pair,
For them its a joy, for us despair.
They're all out in the morning, arranged like
soldiers,
Ready to be scrubbed, and given a proper shower.
Then comes the holiest ritual of all,
When they are dried and kept in as before.
By chance if a shoe is broken, or is ill as she says,
The shoemaker earns in a single go what he couldn't in
hundred
We could almost kill ourselves,
Seeing her shoes' astronomical bill.
Once,

She was prepared to kill her poor little sister
Who'd worn her shoes to the market
As they were meant to be worn on the carpet.
Now miles away, I run off from them,
When I spot them lying in the sun.
Being allergic to dust, she thinks her shoes are too.
When she is sad, the shoes seem to get the blues.
And when they're ready to be discarded,
She feels as sad.
After immense persuasion when she agrees to throw them
away,
And even before we could exclaim 'Thank heavens!'
there's another pair on its way.
They bring her joy, as well as pleasure,
Her only precious treasure.
Take this in from me, my friend,
To win her heart, just start a new trend
To gift her nought but a pair of shoes.

Funskool

All those who claim to love their schools,
Given a chance, would be the first to break the rules.
And for all those shouting 'Miss, Miss, Miss',
The end of school is eternal bliss.
The greatest school patriots
Are perhaps the biggest hypocrites.
Here is an example—
They would like the school to be.
Four periods in all, one for studies
Three for learning how to shout.
The one allotted to studies,
Must not pertain to Physics, Biology, Chemistry
But Vogue, Filmfare or Time.
And examination questions should run like this,
Who's having an affair with Madhuri, Sanjay, Sly or Liz.
As to the principal,
Our God, of whom we can't be critical,
He should be none other than,
Arnold Schwazenegger.
Teasing a girl in class,
Should invite the principal to exclaim,

There's good news for you, enjoy yourselves, be merry,
You'll get an award for this act of bravery.
All those who with their tricks and games,
Make the teachers go insane,
Would be granted a trip to Paris in a plane.
And the class, which creates the maximum havoc and commotion,
Should at the weekend be served with a special Luncheon.'
Friends, all this that I have said,
Is a fraction,
Of what the students would like their school to be,
A paradise, where they can be free.
A long cherished dream come true.

Nature

Darkness, Rain, Thunder,
From where do they come,
You sometimes wonder.
They'll tell you why, they'll give you reasons,
And explain why there is a change in Seasons.
Yet all people who are strictly logical,
May be devoid of a heart, of feelings which are essential
To touch and feel the wonders of Nature,
To dwell in its beauty, to understand each creature.
The raindrops falling are not of water made
For a lover, but teardrops of his parted mate—
The rainbow stretched across the blue
Signifying success for those who have worked and succeeded
Perceiving a leaf shriveled,
An old man may feel quite withered.
And so everything in nature
Is God's message in some way or the other,
There are some who understand,
While others don't bother at all.
But next time you see the first showers of rain,
You don't really have to exert your brain

To understand why it's there,
You should know it's a gift from God
To whom you are so very dear.

Living for Today

Confusion strikes,
You've guessed right.
Guests have arrived
Chaos in the house,
Worried is the spouse.
The last day of the month,
This could be worse than a battle front.
There's hardly any money, but the guests cannot be
    shunned.
In this gloomy picture, there is a bright spot though.
Peace is restored to the couple who have been fighting,
Until their friends come in.
There is joy, laughter, on every face a grin,
The little troubles of life all lost,
Forgotten is the party's heavy cost,
Everyone enjoys as if there were no tomorrow,
As if there were no sadness, no sorrow.

Without Him

Sometimes in life don't you wonder, as I often do,
What would the world be without me and you.
A ghastly thought which often strikes, it would
Be a barren land, no trace of life.
No snow-capped mountains, no streams,
Flowing through valleys and meadows green,
No nightly songs of the sweet nightingale,
Whose voice echoes through the land
Singing how lucky we are to have a life at hand.
Look around you, your family, your friends,
What would have life meant for you
Had they not been around?
To help you, cheer you when in blues.
And what would you do, finally, were there no God,
No creator, no preserver, no saviour,
No one to ask forgiveness from, for the wrongs you do.
No one to believe in, no one to trust whole-heartedly,
When deceived by man,
Without love, compassion, caring,
Without the most important fact of 'sharing'.
Friends lets get together to live like one big family,
Where all disputes could be dealt with calmly.

Magic Valentines

The sheer magic of this day,
Makes the heart sing and be gay.
Even a little smile, a harmless glint in the eye,
Could mean a lot,
Brighten one's life so dull so dry.
Till Valentine's Day, When full of love and cheer,
All the young to each other are dear,
Having waited for this day throughout the year
To express undying love for her,
Don't lose heart if she says no,
Instead of you, your friend she has chosen,
Take her as a fool who by rejecting you
Girls, for you too this is a lovely day,
Open your heart out to him,
Say what you want to say,
Today if you don't speak up, are not bold,
Fuming, fretting, waiting,
You'll only grow into an old maid.
Take him in your arms and wink,
What if you look unwise,
Practice women's liberation day today,
Do and say, what lovers are so shy to.

A fabulous chance for everyone on Earth,
To spread love, to remove all hatred.
A chance for you to choose a partner,
And I promise you,
On this magical, mystical day, no one will refuse!

Unwanted Guests

You're about to sleep, all your work being done,
When suddenly there is a loud noisy horn.
You peep through the window
To see who is there,
Oh! they are guests,
People you just can't bear.
Unwanted guests, intruding onto your shores,
And you were not informed even an hour ago,
In your heart you exclaim 'Oh what a bore!'
But with a huge smile receive them at your door,
For you cannot make the message clear
That you did not want them at any cost here.
Taking your sweet gestures to be true,
They'll reach next time, when the night is half way
    through.
And while they munch,
On your delicious biscuits,
Your tensions keep returning,
At last feeling listless
After about an hour or so,
When they are all ready to leave,

Your daughter may pop up with a game
They don't know how to play,
Yet stay back all the same,
And you wonder how you've saved yourself
From going insane.
A spanking is what she'll get
At last when the game is over,
They witness someone snoring,
The host himself fast asleep,
And knew how unwanted was their trip.

Philosophical Uncle

He takes the world to be useless,
For luxuries he has no zest.
He would have retired a long time ago,
But he has a family to support you know.
People like Gandhi and Mandela are fools, he thinks.
Don't make him see reason
He'll surely argue his way out
He's honest in his work, dislikes crooks,
And on spotting them, he gives them dirty looks.
His views are firm, you cannot change them,
If you tried, you'd have to live till 110.
He has two children
Who respect him.
Is thus a part of the world.
Yet he wishes to fly and be free as a bird.
Leave everything and everyone,
Maybe having shot everyone with a gun.
That's my philosophical uncle,
A sweetest person in the whole world.

Best Friend

I am my own best friend,
I have learnt that the hard way,
But I have learnt that anyway.

They said they would be there,
They said they'd stand by me,
But when the hour came,
Their Faces I could not see,

I am joyous, secure,
I've learnt the hard way
I am my own best friend
I've learnt that any way.

Independence Day

Decades ago, the British left and all those Messiahs who
had fought
For freedom are at rest.
On this day the 15th of August, the British flag was
hauled down
And 'Independence Day' heralded
We rejoiced and made merry
And promised to work for the good of the country.
Years have passed, India has no doubt progressed,
And all our leaders are doing their best to save her from
distress.
On this auspicious Day, let's above all, remember our
brave leaders
Who give up their lives, for us all.
Let's pray together,
May their souls, be blessed forever.

You

When often in a sad or pensive mood,
To me some one has been extremely rude,
I sit and gaze, remember those times,
Remember fondly those words and lines,
Which quite sweetly were uttered by you,
They give me joy, I forget my blues,
That is the magic, the aura you posess,
That is the reason why you are the very best.

Phoney Phone

She talks on the phone,
For ages it seems whether in India or in Rome,
And stops only when her dear husband is home.
Parties, sarees, glamour and all,
And who is taking who, out for a ball,
They know everything that's happening in town,
Whether its regarding a black, a white or a brown.
On the phone, she is sweet, your best friend,
But that, friends, is a misleading impression.
Once the receiver is kept down,
She dials Mrs Kulu, your biggest enemy around.
And now your secrets are making a swift round,
And you'll be made to look like a clown.
But all in all, though the phone encourages gossiping,
And leaves poor mean fretting and fuming
Yet there's no discrimination between black, brown
and white
For all she needs is someone to talk to,
Whether he or she is bright or otherwise.

Offer

In life often you feel miserable,
When you have sorrows and trouble,
When you feel shaken and blue,
When you need help, you really do.

Then all the rest may desert you,
But here is a friend who will help you through,
Remain trustworthy and true,
Prove a good friend, as you would want me to.

Smile

Smile, for there is always a way out.
Smile, for there is much to look forward to.
Discard your sorrows, your blues.
Smile, for there is always a friend, a companion true.
Who'll help you out, who'll help you through.
Smile, for the world is at your feet.
The one you long for, you'll soon meet.
Smile, the world is a better place today.
"Never say die," with courage could say.
Smile, for the world has not come to an end,
A new life commences each tomorrow, setting a better,
brighter trend.

A Crush of Sorts

He walks past me, like a whiff of air,
Oh then the heart break!
As he turns his stern gaze on me,
A more exuberant person, is hard to see.
When he addresses you, his eloquent speech,
Leaves me speechless, with wonder.
A quick gesture, a flicker of the eye,
And all you hear from me is a 'sigh'
I eat drink and sleep in thoughts of him,
You'd think I am a crazy person of sorts.
But well you see it's just infatuation,
A ludicrous situation.
When you know he'll never be yours,
You'll never enter his heart's doors.
A smile from him, leaves me aghast,
"He smiled at me, oh at last!"
Thus go on exclamations infinite.
By his presence, in his every sight.
Life nevertheless goes on,
Oh it stops, I forgot to say,
When he finally speaks TO YOU, some day.
The man in question, is the principal of our school,

Now you'd really think I'm a fool,
But then remember, I did say,
I'll get over this crush some day.
And when I do, a new one shall arrive,
To which again, with all my heart I'll strive!!

Metamorphosis

He's called 'Chi' in the class,
You'd think he's after every lass.
But that's not the case you see,
He's as understanding as can be.
But that was not him last year,
He did some naughty things, oh dear!
Troubled, teased and laughed at girls,
Read their cards, persued their letters
But one fine day, a change took place,
He turned a sage, at a sudden pace.
The abusing, staring, ridicule ended,
No longer were girls offended.
He's changed for the better, he really has,
You'd think every girl is his 'saas',
Here's a newly turned leaf for you,
We like him this way, we do.
And assure him of our help and support
In life whenever he is in the blues.

Source

You know the magical word 'Source'?
Without it you are closed all doors,
Without it, shouting you'd go hoarse.
None will listen to one without a source.
I'd gone for an interview for the job of a maid,
A girl less qualified than I said,
"I am clever, having the biggest source
I'll have this job without doing any course.
You see I'm close to the boss".
That day onwards,
I began gathering all possible sources on which I could
lay my hands.
I wouldn't even buy a pin, for instance,
Without the help of Mr. Ray.
Yet though to such an extent,
I was shocked when to this office I went,
Where the Manager, my source's cousin,
Kept me waiting for an odd reason,
Having a source, I deserved to be served last,
Those who didn't were served with class,
That left me absolutely aghast.

But don't worry I said, I have sources a plenty,
Who'd fix this man, though honest and saintly,
Who tried to teach this simple lesson,
Without a source, you'll do your best to learn,
What a dishonest man, could scarce obtain.

Showing the Way

Time has fled, it's flown by
Giving me no space to breathe, to sigh!
To let you know how I really feel;
My thoughts quite sealed.
Here in at last I let my feelings flow,
And dare to tell you all.
How I care for you, I always have, want you
As a friend who's forever mine,
No other things in mind:-
Let's laugh and talk for a while
I long to see your pleasant smile.
Ah, now, the silver line appears,
My fears fly, love draws near.
I'll always treasure you as a friend and guide.
Showing the way as though to a lost little child.

Holidays

Holidays are fun, some say,
But mine are dull and grey.
Don't be too shocked, dear friend,
I quite dislike these days,
Which you may believe are God sent.
All I do is eat, sleep and grow fat,
And spoil myself to turn a rotten brat.
The Nawabs of Lucknow could not have done better
    then I
In getting up at twelve or later.
A heavy meal, then back to bed.
Sitting and gazing into space is what I dread.
In the evening, if a friend happens to drop by,
He would not leave without a cry.
For I make him listen to all my dreams,
For I have slept for ages it seems.
Why don't I do something constructive my mother
    asks
But haven't I been doing that in school, I say.
I watch television or read
Or shop, every minute complaining.
'Life is so dully and so boring,

T.V. and books are a headache,
I want something different, I want a break.
School I guess was better any day,
At least I didn't like a donkey bray
All day,
When the time comes to leave home,
To go back to the hostel, to the dorm.
I exclaim how wonderful the holidays have been,
When I get back to school, the first thing I say,
Is I wish I could have another stretch of these lovely
    holidays.

Being Special

Gradually the leaves of friendship fall,
Lovingly I pick them all.
Today, tomorrow and all my life through,
I'll remember I knew someone as special as you!

The loving look, the fetching smile,
Makes me feel so special, so liked.
I know I've found a friend in you,
I know there is someone to help me through.
But have I ever told you so,
Did I ever let you know
You're so very special to me
The way you'll always be!

Gautam's B'day Present

She walks in beauty like the night
Of cloudless chimes and starry skies
But she's no Byron's cousin,
Not one in a million, but just a dozen.
She's dark but with huge bright eyes.
With a poor fellow, struck by her,
Looks at her and sighs,
And mutters, 'Be mine honey',
She promptly says, "Not till you have money sunny"
Her gait is slender, sleek,
And when,
Confronted by a wealthy bum
To him her very soul she'll bare.
So beware,
A limousine hates to be compared.
What present shall I buy you on your Birthday
With no money on me?
Let me only say
When you finally do ride in a limousine
Don't overlook your ol' friend Gunjan.

Growing Up

She thought she knew all the answers.
She thought she was a trend setter.
Ardently she wished he'd like her.
And when she wished, he'd write her a letter.
And she wished, he'd be her hero.
But he drifted far away,
He once had made her life,
He now had ruined her days.
And when she longed for a friend,
She indeed got much more,
He knocked and knocked and struck again.
But closed remained her heart's door.
Oh when will you turn old and wise,
Get rid of your squeal, enormous in size.
Perhaps that day would never come,
Perhaps you're sweet as you are,
A little wise and extremely dumb.
But questions will change, as will fashion
That she had grown up, was yet an illusion.

Education: For The 'Privileged' Few

With an entry so lavish and grand,
They came to conquer our motherland.
The British with their cunning brains,
They had little to lose, and much to gain,
Gold, silver, women and all,
The Indian headed for a downfall.
Like slaves they worked from morn to sunset,
In sweat soaked wet.
Education the essence of life,
The very spirit's guide
Was denied to one and all.
Our ancestral lives were full of pathos.
A day came the sahibs realized,
They had to be just free of bias
So they rendered education to the common Indian
On the lines of colleges in England.
Were there hidden flaws?
Indeed they had selfish motives enacting their laws.
Our people made to do tedious calculations,
They sat back and plundered the fruits of their labour.
The wealthy Indians alone could afford
Schools which the poor were hidden

Leading to obvious class distinctions.
Destruction, misery, chaos,
No strings left to pull, none at all.
It's been 40 years or more,
Since they left our country's shores,
Their education systems continue to date,
To hamper and kill all initiative.

First Experience of a Magical Touch

The magical touch, the wonderful charm,
Which works for broken hearts like balm.
If you think you're a sage, there's something amiss,
Your are a teenager, who from her lover has not
received a kiss.
At the very mention of the word, she blushed a deep
red,
"Oh no, not until I'm wed".
But one fine day as he pulled her close,
No questions asked, no dramatic pause.
Just a kiss, and a loving touch,
It left her shocked, Oh! very much.
Terrified she was, extremely grieved,
She thought it was a crime as too a sin.
She howled and wailed, "he loves me no more,
'he'll drop me, label me an utter bore".
But Oh! Behold, the very next hour,
From her lover, she received a flower.
And all those thoughts, "I won't do it again ever",
Like resolutions of the new year,
Faded in oblivion, for ever and ever.

Lets say 'Amen' and end it here,
In future if you meet a girl,
Who exclaims 'Oh dear',
You know what she's been through and done,
And you're sure she cannot be labeled a 'nun'!!

Marital Ads

They mean a lot to some,
To me they mean nothing.
The promises with which they seek to lure you,
Are seldom true.
No, not politicians, nor movie stars,
Not even the clever bania or the local netas.
Will make such tall promises
As the marital ads.
These have quite conveniently flooded the entire
nation.
A green card holder the groom-to-be,
May be as rich as you desire.
When however you take your young daughter there
A man not less than 50 may confront thee.
And when they state the bride-to-be is tall,
And fair and slim and sleek,
They may have forgotten to mention,
She is also anaemic,
Her chances of survival bleak.
A loving caring 'bahu' is all they expect,
But that is for the papers,

You may well know what comes next,
A long list of items,
Which they chose not to mention.
If you cannot afford these,
You cannot rope in their son of course.

Five Years After

High on a wandering Pedestal,
He rides about the town,
A smile to mark his face,
With not a single frown!
Five years have just flown by,
The ponderous gait differs
From the one that *then* was shy.

He set out on a purpose,
To serve those who had endured,
But when the money flowed in,
His 'self' then felt too lured,
Seated in his parlour,
Sipping (slurping) *that,* which he banned
He talked and laughed at a pitch
That ensured he was a 'man'.

And when the sundry came pleading,
He chewed his food and *rose,*
"I have no time for thee' he spoke,
"Do walk out of the door".

He listened though with care,
To what his spouse said
He wouldn't want to upset her,
Lest she disclosed his secret affair.

And thus passed those glorious years,
That numbered in all five—
Now so exhausted was he, that out
Escaped a sigh,

"What pleasure have I derived,
Almighty due to you,
May I serve the people thus,
In life after life!"

His doors are now all open
He's at their feet again,
In case you haven't guessed,
We are talking here,
Of the *evergreen* Indian politician!

For My Sister

When life is lone and Blue,
When you need friends who are true,
When you need a loving smile,
Then you don't have to look a mile,
Just know we are always there
We will all your Burden Bear,
Your heart is pure and sweet
Cruel people you will meet
Keep those lovely eyes open
Not your heart but
Use your head when in need,
My little vulnerable sister
Life is full of sorrow and blisters
Be "Sunny" but keep in mind,
The darkness that lurks behind.
Love is on the way,
You will find it someday,
And when you finally settle
Don't forget Pandi, your sister
And the pathetic poem she wrote
For the most wonderful Person
In this universe remote

Preparing For Examination

We know it is time to get back to our books
Could'nt we just make a living,
By being crooked crooks?

"Wake me up at eleven", shouts one from across
It is past twelve, but she would not budge,
Not by sheer–force, not even if given electric shocks,
"I need a break, I really do", cries another,
Had'nt she been on one, you wonder,
Was'nt she munching, singing and listening to music
She tells you her mind was still in her books,
Oh Lord! We have a genius on our hand it looks!

She is cool, collected and clam,
Prepared? You'd shout out,
She has just given up,
She knows there is more to life,
Than these stupid Exams.

"How much have you done"?
That is a standard one.
Even more standard is the reply

"I am going to fail",
If you are wise you will know,
That is a lie

And then there is me,
If this piece brings a smile,
It is most wanted feeling,
The most desired sensation,
I know I have passed,
Without even sitting for the examination.

Cellular Phones

It is here, there and everywhere,
It is the newest kid on the block,
It adds glamour to your diminishing status,
It is hep, hep, it is the latest,

Ah! You guessed it, I am talking
About the cellur phones spreading
Faster and quicker than viral,
Congectivitis and malaria, all together.

You have the Lala
In his air conditioned Seinna,
There is a call,
The windows roll down,
His face bears a frown,
Is he really speaking,
Or is he pretending
It is cellular phonnenon,
I know it is spreading,

Then there is my brother,
He sat for a puja (prayers)
The cellular on the plate,
It was "inauguration" day,
The offerings were made,
No not to the deity
That was not likely,
Such was the obsession
With the God sent
The snaps that were clicked,
Did not even feature his girl-friend.

Trust

I think I cannot Trust,
Therefore I cannot,
People talked there
Where my soul I did bare

So is it just me?
Or is it people too?
Or is this world a farce?
With friends very few.

If it is a secret,
Keep it to yourself,
Or ask God,

For a helping hand,
When the world turns a fiend
You know you still have two-friends

Jesus Christ

There is Chime in the air,
And it seems to be there,
There is love all around,
It is that lovely sound,
Rejoice, for he's here,
Dear 'O' Dear
God's Chosen one is here,
Christ the saviour
Is here,

Beautiful Day

The day is sunny,
Windy too,
Is it a beautiful day?
Is that cliched?
Beauty Changes
Just as the beholder,
The servant and the master,
A beautiful day will reign for ever
And you will see,
A beautiful day will beautiful always be

Wishful Thinking

I wish those childhood days were mine,
And that I could just stop the time,
I would pick on flowers and butterflies,
I would never be ashamed,
There would be no lies.

The tranquility would always reign,
And innocence would be my game
I would laugh and dance and be MYSELF,
In beautiful dreams forever dwell,
Perhaps these days are just as well,
Perhaps when old and nearing death,
I will have some youthful tales to tell.
And on my table, teeth set in line,
I'd mutter
"I wish those youthful days were mine"

To My Mom

There is just one thing I would like to say,
On this your Special Day,
Among all the Moms I have even seen.

You are the most beautiful,
Most loving and precious,
That could ever have been.
When I have a daughter
Like you do,

I will be her best friend,
And try to be like you.
But she still won't be as blessed
Because I have you
I have the best.

From Me to Him

I like you more and more each day
There are words I keep
And words I say
Its all there in the eyes you know
I love (oops!!)/hate you-it only grows

Since most your statements/compliments
Are followed quite predictably
By a 'but'-here's one of mine
But
I'd like it more if you wore a smile
And not a frown
A t-shirt, not a shirt
Perhaps disclose your liason with me to them (All
your ex's)
And prove yourself less of a flirt
Keep a check on all those "R's" (r, r, r, —)
And read a little more
Perhaps I sound like a bore
Too bad! That's what you apparently fell for

—And of course those jokes
sigh! I bear them everyday
they rather suit the crazy kids
listening religiously to 'jus fo kix'

Again, if you were not an owl
And slept on time each day
You'd reach here spic n' span, in time (not 4.30 pm)
on my most awaited—Sunday

That sums it all I guess
Now,
Do you hate me more, and like me less?
Well, here's the bottom line—
I wouldn't have you change at all
I mean each word I say
Coz you did what none so far could do
You took my heart away.

He

I met a stranger
He said to me,
"For you I have plans galore"
And when I asked him what they were
He said,
"I don't want you to know"
"Alright" I said, "then walk with me
'I have my own plans too
beg you may, and plead with me,
I wouldn't tell you."
But as we walked, I must confess
His kind gaze softened my heart
I told him I wanted to fly
Before the sky grew dark.
We walked, and I felt lost
He showed me my dream path
And when those pebbles on the way
Bit into my weary feet
He lifted me and carried me
In the blazing heat
But when we reached my take off point
Alas, it was dark

I broke down and wept and cried
His way had stalled my flight.
'And why so cruel, so suddenly?
I asked him with a sigh
He said he couldn't answer me
He couldn't tell me why
But if I rose and walked again
And tried with all my might
He would, soon, give me wings to fly.
I asked him what was his name,
Did he treat all the same?
He raised his collar, drew a smirk,
A smirk, I so well knew
'I'm LIFE, he said and added then
'I can be kind and cruel
And when you think I'll give you joy
I can give you the blues'
And with those words he flew away
Bidding me hasty adieu.

At Peace With The Creator

He crept up silently behind
He had no shame at all
We gazed, I tried to read his mind
Between us there was no wall.

All these years I thought I knew him well
As did He too apparently
He played the guiding angel when
My soul I stood to sell.

He held my hand
I was at peace
My soul at once could fly
Beyond the oceans and the land
Tranquility was high

A rendezvous with the Creator
Left me with a contented sigh
For this pleasure, I didn't lie at all
I had only to DIE!

Mountains

When men and mountains meet
Great ideas are conceived.
And though fools do not like to think,
They are compelled to think.
Peace pervades and silence rules.
You search your heart in solitude,
There it is, your only tool.
And when you go down memory lane,
There is lament, there is pain.
But those towering shadows there will comfort you,
Urge you to dare
To look at the world as it does at once
With towering strength and open arms
So when you do go high up there
To leave your grieving soul bare
And get that much elusive peace
Free, not on lease
Then do not throw these peels and wraps
For if these hills turn raging bulls
Where will you go to cleanse your soul
Where will you go to meet with God
Perhaps to his very own abode!

Wisdom

In all those sleeping hours,
When happiness held my hand,
I stood so straight, no bends,
I thought HE was my friend.

And now when I am awake,
With sadness by my side,
I wonder what is at stake,
Perhaps HE is here for wisdom's sake

This is to Us

Just to tell you
That I'm always there
And I know you're there for me too
This is all about you
Your dreams, your thoughts and your expressions
I believe in you—
I believe in them too

This is to us—forever.

The Flower

He saw a pretty flower,
He plucked it and he gazed,
He smiled and thought aside,
I will keep it all my days.

The flower began to wilt,
He had a saddened look,
He'd save the flower he vowed,
He'd try every trick in the book.

He drew a flower on white,
And cheered himself a bit,
He filled this one with colours,
And nursed the 'real' to health.

The colours came to life,
The 'real' flowers stood aside,
Those colours filled his life,
He quite forgot his strife.

He quite forgot but not so,
He went to the 'real' one though,

At times he went to feel good,
Like an old man to his childhood.

So who does he now gaze,
And love with all his might,
Whom does he go to,
You would like to know as I do.

But I am just another flower,
With my own little strife,
And not the penning poet,
Who wrote this terrible slight.

Beyond Sorrow

In life often you feel miserable
When you have sorrows and trouble,
When you feel shaken and blue
And need help you really do.
Then all the rest may desert you,
But here's a friend who'll help you through.
Remain trustworthy and true,
Proving a good friend, as you want me to.

Personality of wet sand
Will tell you this:
        Health is natural, disease unnatural.
Love is natural, hate unnatural
Joy is natural, pain unnatural
Life is natural, death unnatural.

In times of sorrow,
When life to have no purpose or aim,
Remember fondly those precious times,
When apt words and soothing lines,
Were said by someone, loving and caring
By a special friend, who one rarely finds.

When often in a sad or pensive mood,
Someone's been extremely rude.
I sit and gaze, remember those times
Remember fondly those words and lines
Which sweetly were uttered by you
Giving me joy and happiness true.
O the magic, the aura you possess,
Making you indeed the very best.

Teenage Trauma

Softly he said, "I want to go around",
And left me.
I followed her advice, which I thought was sound.
To stay cool.
The former was a guy, the latter a girlfriend,
Both have brought me to a dead end.
I am in a fix, in an absolute dilemma,
I've never experienced such trauma.
Right from the start, I knew I was wrong,
But thought I'd be okay, as time passed on.
A 'sentimental fool' I turned out to be,
The moment I spotted him, somewhere close to me.
I cried, I wept, I dreamed of romance,
His thoughts often put me in a trance.
Then came a jolt, a good one at that,
I spoke to my parents, which made me really glad.
I hardened a little, cried no more,
And almost forced myself to think.
The whole thing was a bore.
I'm back to normal now,
Sensible, mature,

You'd almost think I have no troubles anymore.
But that's not where it ends,
My liking for the guy is like changing trends.
I like him so much now, and hate him so much at
times,
I can't leave him, no, that would be a crime.
Thus life goes on, treading a forked path.
Whoever helps me now, would get all my love.
But if it is a boy, a guy, or a man,
He'd better keep away as far as he can.
For I've had enough of heartache I assure you,
A guy will not get my love for another century or two.

Bookmark

He stood there gazing at the door,
He thought she'd pass him by,
He caught a glimpse and let out a sigh
His love was meant to die!

Happiness

Happiness is inside me,
I have searched,
And it is true.
Search and you will find it too.
Sadness is misty morning,
Giving way to freshest morning dew

THOUGHTS

God

Why do I feel closer to God? I feel like I am attending the "School" all over again. Every day is a new lesson to be learnt. That is probably why I feel closer to God too. I meet Him every day and He is kind to me. He is the perfect "teacher" one never had in school! I quite like this "school". You are allowed considerable freedom in thought and speech etc. God has chalked out a time-table too, but there is scope for changes especially if you are a good student. Most people attend this school when they have left every other tangible school behind. I am a young entrant here. I think God quite likes me.

September 1999

Illusions

Sometimes a picture turns out prettier than the original object. Life—Sometimes a replacement or a less favourable situation can bring colour to your life.

The Sunset today looked like a picture. It looked unreal, too perfect. A picture would have looked more real.

Hope

Think of the best and good will happen to you.
Think of the bad and worst will happen to you.

Introspection

There are enough reasons to get depressed. There are also many reasons I should be smiling. I just have to look harder to find the latter. External factors, it is all an illusion and it is all in the mind. Look for happiness and you will find it. Look for sadness and it will grab you – throttle you till you choke! It is a cling-on, trust me. Also donot depend on external factors to make you happy. Find happiness inside yourself. It is all there in the mind. External factors are a big let down. But that smile there – It is always there and it is always calling out. It is there for grabs – Grab It!

November 1999

Adversity

God gives you suffering but He also gives you strength to bear, fight and eventually overcome the suffering. Nothing comes easy they say. The strength that you need to fight your suffering lies deep inside you. Look for it. Dig deep inside your soul. You will find it.

November 1999

Mirror

Wide eyed wonder – I watch aeroplanes fly just like a small child would. My nose sticking to the window-panes. Suddenly it is not the aeroplane that matters, it is the mist formed on the pane (with my garlic breath). I look at it, write on it. Then I catch a girl staring at me. All at once I am wearing a scarf, I am puffy, without eyebrows – suddenly I am 23 and I am a grown up, a selfish human being.

May 2000

Changing Life

Just spotted a man with pink trousers in the hospital. Trying to imagine history behind the making of these trousers. He must have bought the material or perhaps been gifted the pink stuff by his girl friend. Tailor, Trials fitting etc. The excitement at finally being able to flaunt the pink pair.

They are a bit faded now. Life is like that.

August 2000

Food

Never, ever, disrespect food. I remember once Papa threw a plate of food. Obviously he had been provoked. But I know that I will never do that. Once the food disrespects you and discards your body, you would not know what hit you.

November 1999

Strength

Sometimes I am amazed at my own strength. I could go to a fashion show today with a few strands of hair and still not feel too bad about it. God gives me my strength. But then I wonder how much different my behaviour might have been in this situation. I could either have cried, howled, have been miserable all along or. . . . I am happy because it is the best option available. I want to look happy so that my family feels happy, and when they feel happy I feel genuinely glad. Got it?

October 1999